wearing winter gray (or secrets I learned from the dead)

Lee Clark Zumpe

Wearing Winter Gray
Lee Clark Zumpe

All rights reserved. No part of this book may be reproduced or transmitted in any form or by any means, electronic or mechanical, including photocopying or recording or by any information storage and retrieval systems, without expressed written consent of the author and/or artists.

Wearing Winter Gray is a work of fiction. Names, characters, places, and incidents are products of the author's imagination. Any resemblance to actual events or persons, living or dead, is entirely coincidental.

Poem copyrights owned by the author.
Cover illustration and design by Marcia Borell

First Printing January 2024

Hiraeth Publishing
P.O. Box 1248
Alamogordo, NM 88310
e-mail: hiraethsubs@yahoo.com

Visit www.hiraethsffh.com for online science fiction, fantasy, horror, scifaiku, and more. Stop by our online Shop for novels, magazines, anthologies, and collections. **Support the small, independent press...and your First Amendment rights.**

acknowledgements

"a flurry of sirens" appeared in *The Stray Branch*, Winter 2020
"kitchen ghost" appeared in *The Gloaming Magazine*, Fall 2011
"mastication" appeared in *The Dark Krypt*, Vol. 3, Issue 4
"Nergal and Ereshkigal" appeared *Dreams & Nightmares*, February 2013
"Ullikummi" appeared in *Black Petals*, Issue 27, 2004
"parlor tricks" appeared in *Bete Noire*, Issue 8, August 2012
"witch cult" appeared in *Cast a Curse*, Atlantean Publishing, 2017
"scrying" appeared in *Horror Carousel*, Issue 3, 2005
"the tingling" appeared in *Black Petals*, Issue 26, 2004
"unnamed cemetery" appeared in *Lunatic Chameleon*, Issue 1, 2002
"the vine-covered cabin" appeared in *Wicked Hollow*, Issue 3, 2002
"up at catfish creek" appeared in *Black Petals*, Vol. 5, Issue 4, 2002
"what the cat dragged in" appeared in *Black Petals*, Issue 31, 2005
"Oradea" appeared in *Horror Express*, Issue 2, 2004
"Mount Moldoveanu" appeared in *Dust Devil*, 2002
"Kraków" appeared in *Horror Express*, Issue 5, 2005

table of contents

i.
inexplicable shadows

a flurry of sirens
replay
the blasphemous clock
long, cold winter
intersection
gray with phantoms
kitchen ghost
dissolution
blend right in

ii.
gods & monsters

mastication
Nergal and Ereshkigal
Ullikummi
parlor tricks
witch cult

iii.
haints & hollows

done
scrying
the tingling
unnamed cemetery
the vine-covered cabin
up at catfish creek

iv.
collected cruelties

the taint of depravity
the charity of neighbors
suburban altar
spawning grounds
scrapbook
what the cat dragged in

v.
peppermints and bone marrow

at the door
this road
such delicacies
she shuddered
Oradea
devotion
dawn
dark spheres
bound by the night

vi.
spectral dust

scraps
sycamore
portrait of a filthy alley
Mount Moldoveanu
Kraków
El Chichon
dark wishes

dedication

For Tim Waller, Cynthia Braunstein, Mary Bryant, Mary Jane Dameron, Connie Obrien, & Sarah Allen

i.
inexplicable shadows

a flurry of sirens

a flurry of sirens and flashing lights
       and the muffled voices of neighbors
flocking on driveways
like tittering old crows come October.

a strand of yellow tape
       initially stretched taut,
now drooping languidly
like Christmas trimmings in mid-January.

a crowd of visitors clutching flowers
       and reciting memories,
now a weedy plot negated from consciousness
like lonely schoolyard playgrounds in
midsummer.

a flurry of inexplicable shadows
       and hushed whispers after midnight
reflecting an abridgment of the living years
like a lackluster eulogy hastily composed.

replay

Imagine inescapable solitude.
The ultimate expanse of
growing indifference.
Cyclic conduits provoking
candid appraisals,
replaying each discrepancy
with the mute torment of
accuracy. A shadow
of life, an echo of an
inconsequential existence, confined to
a formless miasma of
spectral construct, obliged
to retrace an immaterial lifetime
of missteps, regrets and misery.

the blasphemous clock

the blasphemous clock stands in
    the shadowed corner
tallying up all the wasted moments
in the buzz of obsolete hours;

impatiently truncates protracted passages
punctuating pages as the chapters
grow tiresome and pointless;

chronologically predisposed, our course is
strict –
governed by innate limited perception
and finite parameters of our own obtuse
    design;

beginning/middle/end, birth/life/death:
a jumble of abstractions set against the
    black abyss
of self-inflicted limited immortality.

long, cold winter

I left her there,
shimmering like
last winter's bleached bones
splayed out across April.

I left her there,
lingering like
polished cairn stones
so meticulously arranged.

I left her there,
glistening like
dew shortly after dawn
on the cusp of mourning.

I left her there,
retreating like
the Arctic sun anticipating
a long, cold winter.

intersection

the ivory light of an anxious moon
highlighting the rough edges

of aging gravestones
where silver orbs wing
unseen amidst dutiful caretakers.

the grainy dust of gradual disintegration
ground underfoot
along the narrow paths
skirted by weedy patches
and wind-strewn flowers.

the paralysis of communal grief
intersecting with hope
where memories linger
with a ghostly conscience
beneath a shadowed steeple.

gray with phantoms

In certain moments rooted
    deep in the nucleus of darkling hours
Where lovers forsake individuality
    and merge in body and in mind and in spirit;
In hidden spaces and in sacred places
    beneath the aura of the waking world
Where the air is gray with phantoms
    and sweet with the perfume of innocence;
Where the concept of life and death disintegrates
    and time flows cyclically;
Where artists' brushstrokes color the cosmos
    and poets' verses kindle souls into being —

The warmth of distant passions and lingering sentiments
    calm the worn and weary travelers on their long journey.

kitchen ghost

butterfly memories
flutter like whispers of the dead
beneath the white rasp of kitchen lights

crimson droplets
assemble along the countertop
tiny as baby toes

serrated kiss
of a stainless-steel lover
and the deceitful promise of silence

wedding-gift silver
jangles in midnight drawers
while cupboard doors shudder

neglected faucet
weeping into dishwater
like incessant suicide tears

dissolution

I feel it pressing downward,
the ponderous star-flecked sky,
as I reluctantly recede,
withdrawing into this dank asylum –

this temporary sanctuary
beneath the sodden earth,
as somber pallbearers
whisper sincere elegies.

a coin is fixed upon my tongue
that I might offer brooding Charon
in the hope that he deliver me
across the boiling river Acheron.

blend right in

made from material collected
from our surroundings,
we usually blend right in,

remaining unnoticed for the
duration. Moss will grow,
they say, like long-ago summer days;

sprouting tumors overnight,
belated souvenirs from rowdy
childhood antics. Wearing winter

gray, we try to wash it all away,
dulling the perceived sharpness
and understating the value.

ii.
gods & monsters

mastication

another fallen angel,
casualty of Lucifer's eternal war,
butchered on the battlefield of Earth.

severed into her tattered bits,
she loses that seraphic charm;
still, she is one of cultivated taste;

frothing hungry wolf, hard-pressed
to stay his paws – licking his lips
and gnashing his jaws.

fleshpots for the fastidious appetite –
machinations of an epicurean devil:
to the victor go the spoils of war.

Nergal and Ereshkigal

I dreamt of loutish Nergal in the netherworld,
officiating some dire conference in Aralu
under the attentive eye of his beloved
    Ereshkigal –
her flesh lustrous with the radiance of fresh
    corpses.

The words of his sermon whirred like swarming
    honeybees,
his droning fanaticism a gummy web of
    alluring entanglements
calculated to capture the interest of the darkest
    gods ...
for this necropolis housed a pantheon of
    discarded deities.

He articulated her pledge of timely resurrection
his fiery words spawning thunderous applause
amongst the legions of the dead, shadow-eyed
    and dutiful;
their fervent ecstasies echoed upward through
    the seven gates.

I dreamt of ancient ruins shrouded by the
    sediment of history,
silver moon-glow sparkling against time-worn
    monoliths,
buried tombs of long-forgotten kings and
    neglected temples
where Ereshkigal once received mortuary
    offerings.

Ullikummi

you with your pit-candle
chanting incantations
      from some obsolescent lexicon
while the basement floor dissolves,
soul swallowed down the long
      black throat of the earth
where the stone-god Ullikummi,
fossilized in mid-season,
      poster boy for botched vengeance,
lingers amidst Milton's sights of woe,
where each word from your lips
      is a pickaxe chipping granite.

parlor tricks

So parlor tricks simply
won't cut it any longer,
all the cliché antics that won
applause and astonishment

amongst the Spiritualist crowd
lack luster captured in
the surreal bottle-green world
of night-vision footage.

Kate and Margaret,
your successors come
armed to the teeth,
intent on collecting concrete evidence:

infrared thermometers,
digital cameras and audio equipment
have supplanted the Ouija-reading,
séance-holding, table-tipping Fox sisters.

In shadowed, quiet places,
amidst the skewed stones
of forgotten burial grounds,
they wait for the film crew:

these weary haunters weave
electronic voice phenomena,
practice conjuring light anomalies
and dream of television stardom.

witch cult

Their antics amused Keziah,
    at least for a while:
Girls, hungry for affection,
repressed and craving attention,
playing out fantasies,
invoking truly mortal demons:
    Fear and *Vengeance*.

Silly things, really,
    given to fits of madness:
With wicked imaginations
They conjured droll horrors,
Envisioning witch cults;
When they fingered Keziah
    she stopped cackling.

Good thing Brown Jenkin
    knew his stuff:
He made certain
Salem would not burn her;
She left behind only shadows
and geometric puzzles
    to befuddle Mr. Mather.

iii.
haints & hollows

done

      it's done.
the weeping, the shouting,
the carrying on at all hours – done.

      I know
by the desperate shadows squirming
against the drawn blinds
and nicotine-stained curtains
of the double-wide;

      I know
by the crash of the porch door
sending echoes across the haunted hollows
and weeping coves
of this Appalachian community;

      I know
by the anxious shovel sinking
into the cold earth,
disturbing the sacred soil
of this merciful mountain –
      it's done.

      Only –
when he comes back to fetch me,
to drag me to my unmarked grave,
he'll find I'm not so eager to comply:
maybe he didn't use enough poison –

    Or maybe
grandma, who considered herself a witch,
really does watch over me like Mama said –
either way, death doesn't seem as limiting
as I had anticipated.

So, when he comes back to fetch me,
he'll learn: it's done – but it ain't over.

scrying

scrying in a bowl of jet black water
      with a shard of winter
splintered underfoot;

bleak December frieze outside,
      the icy window frame
on the far side of the solstice;

the mountain coughs up her ghosts
      smothered in frost,
eager for the warmth of conversation.

the tingling

when the first winter of his dead time
subsided
the ice encasing his flesh thawed
and he drowned
just a little.

he had plenty of time
to make excuses
for his predicament:
anything to resist the truth.

when the worms dug in
they found some live nerve endings
and snapped a few neurons.

he came to enjoy the tingling sensation:
it was all he had left,
after all.

unnamed cemetery

indistinguishable:
standing on the weedy southwestern corner
beneath the knotty old oak
(the one locals call Indian Mark),
it neither towers above its grim companions
nor gleams more distinctly
in the noonday sun.

up in the Blue Ridge, under
the yellow poplars,
with winter skulking through
the balsams, the stones
forget their names
and lose their faces.

fastidious fact-tracking genealogists
grumble as they depart empty-handed;
thwarted, they do not realize:
what the markers lack in practical data
they make up for in phantasmal character.

the vine-covered cabin

I remember visiting Uncle Judah
down in Sugarcamp Hollow;
sitting out on the porch
while Daddy split wood;
and Judah would watch us,
sitting tall in his rocking chair,
nothing but coal-black eyes
and a twisting snarl –
too old to do for himself,
too stubborn to leave his shack
Daddy always said.
One winter we stopped going
down to Sugarcamp Hollow –
Daddy said we had no need.
I imagine the Virginia Creepers
have swallowed that cabin
over the years,
but I expect Judah
is still watching us
from his rocking chair.

up at catfish creek

Found her name in the obits one day last week:
A clipped little blurb
Summing up too little
Of the girl I used to meet
Up at Catfish Creek.

Wondered how much they really cared,
The faceless survivors
Who did her no justice
And provided no picture
To memorialize her in print.

Could have said so much more than they did,
Described her beauty
Praised her intellect
Celebrated her academic achievements
Mentioned her recent love interest.

Clipped the text anyway with my favorite pair
of scissors:
With a thumbtack I added it
To the bulletin board in the basement
Where I keep a lock of her hair
I trimmed up at Catfish Creek.

iv.
collected cruelties

the taint of depravity

Old man, skirting the borders of midnight
    with dirty fingers and
    a bundle of stale guilt.

Young woman, face folded in black and white
    with pleas and waning hopes
    recorded in forgotten newspapers.

Unwelcome ghosts – friends, lovers, unborn children –
    colonize the shadows and
    whisper condemnation.

Old man, time cannot sweep from your eyes
    the taint of depravity nor wash
    the blood from your hands.

the charity of neighbors

Delores clamped onto the counter,
looking out over the kitchen sink
through the window box and into the backyard
where Herb, her neighbor from down in the
    hollow,
shambled along the edge of the woods
dragging an axe behind him.
    It was done, then.
The red stains splashed across his
    cotton white tee
contrasted with the oxeye daisies blooming in
    her garden,
and Delores thanked her stars that she did not
    do his laundry.
As he moved along, she saw the lumpy sack
thrown over his right shoulder;
he shifted its weight, once, and an arm
jutted out of a hole, bobbing up and down with
    his gait,
waving at Delores.
    Delores smiled and waved back.
Maybe later Herb would bring her a meat pie
and she could thank him for helping with the
    chores.

suburban altar

long removed, the stars
fester against a specter of mist
drifting drunkenly over the rooftops;

ritual shrugs its habitual trappings
for slapdash insight and enhanced perception,
a muddle of token incantations

and half-invented traditions
simulating ceremony; still, the offering
(found in scabs and morsels

simmering amidst canned veggies
in a pool of broth)
invokes some spectacle at midnight –

the lone practitioner
squats on the kitchen floor
eagerly licking his bloodied chops.

spawning grounds

She dips a finger in her drink, sucks it
seductively,
her playful smile an exclamation point
to the proposition she has just finished
whispering into my ear.

I lay a Ulysses S. Grant on the table, tip
generously,
partially to impress my lusty catch
but primarily because it's hard to find
a decent waitress at a dockside inn.

She demonstrates her skills, performs
dexterously,
as we drive to a remote stretch of beach
where my family's ancestral estate oversees
the Atlantic's erratic moods atop a high cliff.

I take her on a ledge overlooking the sea,
indulge her
copiously,
pleased to find such a lecherous appetite
in a world enfeebled by STDs and the myth
of contemptible monogamy.

She glides along the outgoing tide, floating
effortlessly,
her waning life a vessel for our hatchlings
who someday will heed a similar impulse
and come home to spawn.

scrapbook

*night spreads across the sky
like his shadow swallowing the room;*

through the haze of trauma-tainted memory,
tarnished with years of self-abuse and alcohol,
his lecherous scowl is a snapshot
in my secreted scrapbook –

yellowed pages filled with
a history of neglect and torment,
stapled screams and
decoupage tears –

now, here, before me, the withered remnant
begging my forgiveness
in a silent shudder of indignation
amidst a rats' nest of lines, tubes, and drains –

his malice softened by age and arterial plaque,
twisted fingers trembling;
in his eyes, though, a spark lingers:
sadistic designs and collected cruelties –

*night spreads across the sky
like blood pooling on cold hospital tile.*

what the cat dragged in

Tokens of her affection, they
tell me, scattered throughout
the house; she stands by
contentedly, crimson-lipped,
guarding each monstrous mass
of unidentifiable gore. Initially,
lizards kept her occupied;
their squirming, severed tails
writhing on the porch
long after she had finished
them. Next came birds
with a flurry of feathers;
then mice and larger
rodents fell victim as
she expanded her hunting
grounds. Now, she brings
in mangled bits of meat
and fur and flesh beyond
classification – dragging
mutilated carcasses across
the kitchen tile, ignoring me,
taking them down into
the basement. I mop
the floors daily, eyeing
stains that seem to form
symbols and pentagrams.
I scratch her bobbing head
as she licks her paws,
slick with blood.

v.
peppermints and bone marrow

at the door

Treading lightly within
satiny folds of midnight,
glimmering stars intimate
sharp, stinging agonies,
but fail to divert me.

I linger at the door,
eager but patient;
hungry but apathetic.

Pressing softly upon
preternatural silhouettes,
obliging shadows conspire
to grant safe passage
recognizing a kindred soul.

Her body trembles
beneath the sheets;
sweat blossoms across her brow.

Drifting quietly above
a delectable, alien indulgence –
cuisine conscientiously cultivated,
bioengineered over millennia –
fit for elite connoisseurs.

I savor each morsel,
sweet, succulent, luscious,
as I ingest her luscious soul.

this road

     sometimes
I cannot help but be impatient.

     how could you know
what it is like to perceive
of the aging of distant stars?

     you come to me
with your impure contemplations,
pouting lips dripping with iniquitous
applications
dirty as a heretic's tongue.

     you come to me
thinking you can impress me
with your monotonous observations –
as though I had not experienced
everything you might offer.

     how could you know
what it is like to outlive
entire civilizations?

this road, too, I have traveled.

such delicacies

Such delicacies I can offer you,
she teased a smile onto my grim
and somber face with her funereal charms.

The club pulsated with irksome feral heat
and the vulgarities of common appetites.
Mutually attracted to finer standards
of wantonness, we slipped out the stage door
and down the alley where junkies
curled in embryonic carriages
within the buzz of mundane euphoria.

Such delicacies, she repeated, and in ecstasy
we raped the twilight and polluted sacred
        shrines
and corrupted every susceptible angel,
leading an orgy of profane gratification
amidst a tangle of despoiled flesh and warm,
fresh blood; we teetered on the precipice
just this side of the sanctimonious dawn,
shadows black as crematorium soot
saturating her callous eyes,
her breath an intoxicating mix
of peppermints and bone marrow.

she shuddered

Nothing more than a fluttering of black wings
against a Stygian canopy,
shadow eclipsing shadow,
and she shuddered
and drew the ruffled lace curtains
together.

Nothing more than a wavering of lamplight
across her bedroom chamber,
cold December creeping through,
and she shuddered
and drew the down-filled comforter
higher.

Nothing more than a curdling of images
amidst her gentle dreams
a faceless, winged lover's kiss,
and she shuddered
and drew these hungry crimson lips
closer.

Oradea

snow smothered Oradea,
wilting through
another Transylvanian winter

where the years accumulate
in black and white thumbnails,
naked medieval woodcuts;

streets dotted with
shadow-thin stragglers,
indigenous to twilight,

and incurable victims
eager to surrender their souls
to vampiric designs.

even as crimson droplets
speckle the white powdery floor,
she drowns in regret:

an unrequited lover
on a suicide plunge
longing for her perch.

devotion

My devotion to her
remains unconcealed.

From the murky tarns of twilight
she stirred, black satin eyes
embracing all things
dark and beautiful.

Her impatient suitors,
wild and arrogant,
wrestled with the invidious moon
and possessive stars alike.

Their ancient rivalry
meant nothing to her –
their sycophantic overtures
sparked no hint of desire.

I sat, brooding,
amidst brick-built crypts –
ancient and crumbling –
gargoyles writhing in shadows;

my devotion to her
remains unchallenged.

dawn

A slender orange band
sharpens the edge of the far horizon.
Far-flung stars glimmer,
struggling to hold on to their supremacy
a few precious moments longer.
I watch eagerly as the determined day
drives a million shimmering
stakes through the heart of night.
With ice under my skin,
I fall back into darkness,
and into the comfortless womb
I call home.

dark spheres

> *I heard the trailing garments of the*
> *Night*
> *Sweep through her marble halls!*
> From "Hymn to the Night," Henry
> Wadsworth Longfellow

the elusive strings which compose the cloak of
dusk
beneath her subtle, graceful hands
once spawned music to soothe
our hungry hearts;

the dark spheres outshining our benighted
souls
now boil with storm-tossed furies –
her hunger ebbed and she left me
icy and overcast.

bound by the night

the darkness polluted her eyes –
the blackness burned in her blood.

I found her on the streets
alone, desolate, wounded:
a slave to her addiction,
wandering without destination,
shambling like a corpse
haphazardly reanimated.

I seduced her into my company,
benevolent, considerate, stern:
a redeemer and a mentor,
unfettering her from dependence,
scattering her defects
like bothersome gnats.

I assimilated her with compassion,
impulsive, instinctual, effortless:
a pariah to her own species,
dispossessed and ostracized,
reshaping her genetic composition
to create an exquisite hybrid.

I left her to her own devices,
wolfish, cunning, proud:
an alien appetite embedded,
driven by ravenous hunger,
preying on those who shunned her
with newfound vitality.

the darkness sharpened her eyes –
the blackness fueled her passion.

vi.
spectral dust

scraps

orange grove, long abandoned,
haunted by the fragrance of its detritus.
weedy aisles canopied by spindly limbs;
unseen rodents, foraging through scrub;
insects examining a snake's shed skin.

with the rustle of crows' wings,
twigs snap as I approach
the foundation of a deserted bungalow.
glass shards shimmering in sunlight,
broken bits of tile and porcelain fixtures.

between scattered cinder blocks
and empty terra cotta pots,
a serpentine garden hose
reflexively coiled.
the shadows stretch across decades.

sycamore

I remember – long ago, late one afternoon,
When they came, wearing suits and scowls,
    to the door;
I was waiting there, quietly, alone,
Beneath the boughs of the old sycamore.
I remember – though I was just a little kid;
So many faces I'd never seen before –
Strangers, frightening me; I ran and hid,
Beneath the boughs of the old sycamore.
    They stayed a while and wept, then left for evermore;
    And I wait still, beneath the boughs of the sycamore.

portrait of a filthy alley

twilight ribbon stretches between
the summits of rival tenements.
    televisions bicker,
        spouses squabble.

backdoor lamplights illuminate
mounds of festering garbage.
rodents skirt the ragged glow.
        distant sirens scream.

innumerable cockroaches forage.
stray cats linger on the shores
of putrid wastewater puddles.
        sporadic coughing,
        soft weeping.

malcontents on prolonged sabbaticals
huddle beneath newspaper blankets.
      clanking bottles,
      rattling lungs.

clouds of darkness rise
from wells of neglect and sorrow.
dark gods collect disciples.
      whispered sermons,
      mellifluous invocations.

Mount Moldoveanu

Understand, of course, that things are not what
they once were:
No more screech owls prowling forests hunting
shadow prey;
No more gargoyles preaching from their gothic
perches
      in European haunts;
No more Beltane fires in the highlands.

Some nights I find myself alone on Mount
Moldoveanu,
      trying to peel familiar voices from
October gales;
Some nights the stars mock me.
Some nights the ghosts of dead poets try to
sooth me.

The moon – my adopted sister – lingers along
the horizon
      shunned by the city lights,
Banished like an obsolete folk remedy or an
Old Religion.
I drink a toast to her, and we mourn the world
that withered
      at our feet.

Kraków

As the diluted sun hobbles off the stage
behind the sooty curtain,
emaciated creatures pile into the muddy streets
—
weary and broken, only their eyes betray
    hunger.

Coke ovens stain the twilight furnace-red,
and the howl of prowling machines punctuates
    the night.

A forest of chimneys coughs up the filthy black
    breath
of the tainted earth.

Kraków withers beneath a regime of vampires.

El Chichon

In sleepy San Cristobal,
they shuffled through
the gritty streets
after El Chichon.

I watched them for days,
mere stick-figures,
braving the spectral dusk
at noon-time;

I watched as the gaunt outcasts
choaked on the ash
that smothered their town,
searching for salvation.

Survivors of the upheaval,
their world had become
a pallid ghost.

dark wishes

ancient stars sweep sickened skies
in an endless procession,
disbursing and realigning
in a somnolent ballet

too protracted to be observed,
too complex to be calculated
by all but the most fastidious
and dutiful disciple.

their wan light, cast vast
aeons past, shines feebly
upon crumbling steeples and
narrow cobblestone alleys;

over battlefields and burial grounds
and zealously guarded borders;
across bloated refugee camps
and into homeless shelters;

and on sleepy towns
where chronic apathy,
misplaced prejudice and callousness
breed dark wishes.

about the author

Lee Clark Zumpe, an entertainment columnist with Tampa Bay Newspapers, earned his bachelor's in English at the University of South Florida. His short stories and poetry have appeared in a variety of literary journals, anthologies, and genre magazines. Publication credits include appearances in *Tiferet, Modern Drunkard Magazine, Space & Time, Mythic Delirium* and *Weird Tales*.

Lee lives on the west coast of Florida with his wife and daughter.

www.ingramcontent.com/pod-product-compliance
Lightning Source LLC
LaVergne TN
LVHW010435070526
838199LV00066B/6036